UNSUNG HEROES OF
TECHNOLOGY

by Todd Kortemeier

www.12StoryLibrary.com

12-Story Library is an imprint of Peterson Publishing Company and Press Room Editions.

Produced for 12-Story Library by Red Line Editorial

Photographs ©: Public Domain, cover, 1, 18; Jemal Countess/Stringer/Getty Images, 4; Designua/Shutterstock Images, 5; Agence de presse Meurisse/National Library of France, Prints and Photography Department, EI-13 (2787), 6; Olga Popova/Shutterstock Images, 7; Howard R. Hollem/Office of War Information/Library of Congress, 8, 29; Pablo Martinez Monsivais/AP Images, 9; AP Images, 10, 16; Jim McKnight/AP Images, 12; NASA, 14, 15, 28; Monkey Business Images/Shutterstock Images, 17; Evan-Amos, 20; Heritage Images/Corbis, 22, 25; Home Office/PA Wire URN:24636917/Press Association/AP Images, 23; Guy Erwood/Shutterstock Images, 24; The Washington Times/ZumaPress/Newscom, 26

Library of Congress Cataloging-in-Publication Data
Names: Kortemeier, Todd, 1986- author.
Title: 12 unsung heroes of technology / by Todd Kortemeier.
Other titles: Twelve unsung heroes of technology
Description: North Mankato, MN : 12-Story Library, [2017] | Series: Unsung
  heroes | Audience: Grades 4 to 6. | Includes bibliographical references
  and index.
Identifiers: LCCN 2016002373 (print) | LCCN 2016004732 (ebook) | ISBN
  9781632353115 (library bound : alk. paper) | ISBN 9781632353610 (pbk. :
  alk. paper) | ISBN 9781621434757 (hosted ebook)
Subjects: LCSH: Inventors--Biography--Juvenile literature. |
  Technology--History--Juvenile literature. | Science--History--Juvenile
  literature.
Classification: LCC T39 .K67 2017 (print) | LCC T39 (ebook) | DDC 609.22--dc23
LC record available at http://lccn.loc.gov/2016002373

Printed in the United States of America
Mankato, MN
May, 2016

Access free, up-to-date content on this topic plus a full digital version of this book. Scan the QR code on page 31 or use your school's login at 12StoryLibrary.com.

Table of Contents

Patricia Bath Saves Eyesight through Invention 4

Jagadish Bose Makes Wireless Technology Possible 6

Yvonne Brill Helps Power Rockets into Space 8

Grace Hopper Changes Computer Programming 10

Shirley Ann Jackson Advances Telecommunications 12

Katherine Johnson Charts a Course for the Moon 14

Hedy Lamarr Acts to Help the War Effort 16

Lewis Latimer Assists Thomas Edison 18

Jerry Lawson Helps Invent the Video Game Console 20

Ada Lovelace: First Computer Programmer 22

Alan Turing Invents the Modern Computer 24

James West Lets People Be Heard 26

Fact Sheet 28

Glossary 30

For More Information 31

Index 32

About the Author 32

Patricia Bath Saves Eyesight through Invention

Patricia Bath's interest in science came from her mother. She encouraged her daughter to read and bought her a chemistry set. Patricia's mother was descended from African slaves and Cherokee Indians. Patricia heard stories about people all around the world from her father. He had been a sailor and a newspaper columnist. These stories got Patricia interested in all different kinds of people. She grew up wanting to help people by using science.

Growing up in the 1940s, Bath had to work hard to get where she wanted to go. Some people had racist views about black people. Many also thought that women had no place in the world of science and technology. But Bath's talent was impossible to ignore. By the age of 16, she was winning science awards. She chose a career in medicine and worked her way through school. She specialized in working with eye health, or ophthalmology. In 1974, she became a professor at the University of California Los Angeles. She was the first woman in the ophthalmology department's history.

Bath received a 2012 Tribeca Disruptive Innovation Award, which recognizes individuals who overcame challenges and contributed to society.

4

Bath developed a new way to remove cataracts.

Bath began a successful career in medicine and education. But her lasting contribution to the field was an invention. In 1981, she had an idea for a new type of surgery using lasers. These lasers would be used on cataracts. A cataract is a condition that affects the lens of the eye. Cataracts can cause blurry vision or blindness.

To fix cataracts, a machine makes a tiny cut in the eye. It then removes the damaged lens. Then a new lens is inserted. Using a laser, the procedure would take only a few minutes. Bath designed the new surgery herself, but the technology at the time made it impossible. It took five years of development and research. Then Bath went to Germany to test it with the most advanced lasers.

It took a few more years of testing to get a patent. It was granted in the United States in 1988. Bath's device is in worldwide use today. She considers it her greatest achievement. And restoring sight is her greatest reward.

Cataract

Healthy eye

Clear lens

Eye with cataract

Lens clouded by cataract

30

Number of years a woman in North Africa had been blind before Bath's device allowed her to see.

- Bath became interested in science and people at a young age.
- She went to college to study medicine and became an eye doctor.
- She invented a device that uses lasers to cure cataracts.
- The device is in worldwide use and can restore sight to some blind people.

Jagadish Bose Makes Wireless Technology Possible

Jagadish Bose was born in 1858 in India. At that time, India was ruled by Great Britain. Bose's father wanted to make sure his son grew up knowing his home country. He enrolled his son in a school that taught the local language and culture. Bose read tales of great heroes in India. He was inspired by those who came from nothing but did great things.

Bose went on to a college that specialized in teaching science. He had a strong interest in and talent for physical science. To pursue a career in science, he had to go to England. He earned a science degree from the University of London. But even back in India, he had a hard time getting a job. The British did not think Indians were capable of being professors.

Bose was forced to accept a temporary position at a college in Calcutta, India. He ended up teaching there for 30 years. But he

Bose taught science classes for 30 years.

A German stamp showed Marconi and his wireless telegraph. Bose's work made this invention possible.

was able to continue his research. Bose experimented with radio waves. The idea of sending a signal without wires was a new and exciting concept. Bose created devices that could send and receive these waves. In 1895, he held a demonstration. He could send waves 75 feet (23 m) and through walls.

5

Length, in millimeters, of the radio waves that Bose generated.

- Bose was born and educated in India.
- He studied further in London, then came back to India to teach.
- He did pioneering research into radio waves but never patented any technology.
- Marconi used Bose's research to invent the wireless telegraph.

Italian inventor Guglielmo Marconi used some of Bose's research in his wireless telegraph. He won the 1909 Nobel Prize for it. While Bose's work played a role in Marconi's invention, he never got credit for it. One of the biggest reasons is that Bose never patented his work. He did not have much interest in making money. He simply wanted people to benefit from his discoveries.

BOSE THE WRITER

Bose's interest in science was creative as well. He was also a published science fiction writer. In 1898, he wrote the first work of science fiction in his native Bengali language.

Yvonne Brill Helps Power Rockets into Space

Today, many children are taught that they can be anything they want to be. If you want to grow up to be a rocket scientist, you can work hard and do it. But growing up in Canada in the 1930s, Yvonne Brill was told just the opposite. Brill was a strong student with an interest in math and physics. But none of her high school teachers encouraged her. One even told her that women weren't fit to have careers.

Brill's school principal was slightly more positive. He thought she could be a teacher. But Brill had her sights set on something else. She wanted a career in science. She knew it would be hard to get a fair chance because she was a woman. But during World War II, a lot of men were off fighting. This opened up new opportunities for women.

In 1945, after graduating from the University of Manitoba, Brill moved from her native Winnipeg. She took a job with Douglas Aircraft in California. It's possible she was the only female rocket scientist working

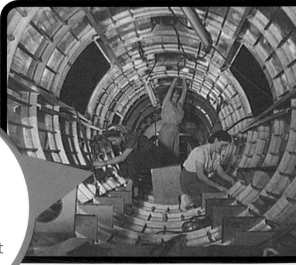

Women helped put together planes for Douglas Aircraft during World War II. Brill worked as a rocket scientist there.

in the United States at that time. She worked mainly on the systems that make rockets go. But her career came to a temporary stop in 1958. She took time off to raise her children.

In 1966, she went back to work on rocket engines. In 1972, she had her greatest achievement working for a company called Astro Electronics. She developed a thruster system to keep satellites in orbit around Earth. The system was first used in 1983. It is still in use today. Around that same time, she also worked on the space shuttle for NASA. The shuttle was a reusable spacecraft.

Brill passed away in 2013. In her last years, she finally received recognition for her achievements. She was inducted into the National Inventors Hall of Fame in 2010. In 2011, President Barack Obama presented her with the National Medal of Technology and Innovation.

5,000
Weight, in pounds (2,268 kg), that Brill's thruster system could move.

- Brill was interested in math and science as a girl. But her teachers did not encourage her in her studies.
- During World War II, she got a job in aviation and started working on rocket engines.
- Brill designed a thruster system to keep satellites in orbit and also worked on the space shuttle.

President Obama honored Brill with the National Medal of Technology and Innovation.

Grace Hopper Changes Computer Programming

Computer science didn't really exist as a job when Grace Hopper started. It certainly was nothing like today. "Computers" more often meant humans who performed calculations that machines could not do. Hopper was at the forefront of computer science when she enlisted in the navy in 1943.

She had been a math professor at Vassar College. But the United States was in the midst of World War II. Hopper wanted to help with the war effort. At 37, she was not a typical naval recruit. But she showed a talent for the work. She was assigned to work on a real computer at Harvard University. Computers at that time were the size of entire rooms.

Hopper worked on early computers.

Hopper's commanding officer was shocked that he was sent a woman. But Hopper proved she belonged. Because of her age, she wasn't allowed to join active duty after World War II ended. But she stayed on as a reserve. In 1949, she went to work for a new company that made computers.

In those days, computers made by different companies could not talk to each other. They all had their own languages. Programmers had to know all these languages to get computers to work. In 1959, Hopper developed a language called COBOL. It stood for Common Business Oriented Language. It allowed computers to communicate with each other. It also allowed people to program computers using plain English.

Hopper retired as an admiral in 1986. By the year 2000, 70 percent of the code running all computers used in business was COBOL.

12,000

Approximate number of attendees at the 2015 Grace Hopper Conference, a gathering of women interested in computer science.

- Hopper enlisted in the navy to help the United States during World War II.
- She got assigned to work with computers.
- Hopper went to work for one of the first computer manufacturers in 1949.
- She developed a universal programming language called COBOL that allowed computers to communicate.

THE USS *HOPPER*

In 1997, the US Navy named a new ship the USS *Hopper*. It was only the second ship named for a woman who had served in the navy. Hopper did not live to see it. She passed away in 1992.

11

Shirley Ann Jackson Advances Telecommunications

It is important that a university president be a good communicator. Shirley Ann Jackson did revolutionary work in communications technology. So it's appropriate that she became the first woman to lead Rensselaer Polytechnic Institute (RPI), a university dedicated to technology research.

Jackson became president of RPI in 1999.

Jackson's parents made her education a priority. She was a strong student. In 1964, she graduated at the top of her class from Roosevelt High School in Washington, DC. Later that year, she started attending the Massachusetts Institute of Technology (MIT). MIT is one of the best colleges in the world. There were fewer than 20 black students there at the time. And Jackson was the only one studying physics.

Jackson had many options for colleges. But she chose MIT to encourage other black students to go there. She was one of only two women in her class to graduate. She stayed at MIT and pursued her PhD. She made history there again. Jackson was the first woman in MIT history to earn a PhD in physics.

Jackson made a name for herself in theoretical physics. Her research focused on what things were made of and what they could do. In 1976, she went to work for

53
Number of honorary degrees Jackson earned for her work in science as of 2016.

- Jackson's parents encouraged her to study science.
- She was one of very few black students at MIT, and one of two women in her class to graduate.
- Jackson's work at Bell Telephone enabled the invention of several telecommunications technologies.

Bell Telephone. She worked in its research department. The company was interested in what materials conducted electricity well.

Her research made a lot of telecommunications technology possible. Based on her work, inventions such as the portable fax machine, fiber optic cables, and caller ID were created. Jackson was inducted into the National Women's Hall of Fame in 1998. In 1999, she became president of RPI.

Katherine Johnson Charts a Course for the Moon

Katherine Johnson loved math from the age of four. Growing up in the 1920s and 1930s, she counted everything she could see. She knew how many steps it was from her house to her church. She didn't know that one day, the distances she'd deal in would be hundreds of thousands of miles.

Johnson's family encouraged her learning. Her father had only a sixth-grade education. But he could solve some math problems that even Katherine's teachers couldn't. Katherine, too, was good at math. She skipped two grades and started high school at age 10. In 1937, she graduated from college at 18.

Johnson was black. Growing up in West Virginia, she did not experience much racism. Her first encounter with it came while she was taking the bus to Virginia for her first job as an elementary school teacher. The driver made her and

Johnson was one of the first black women to work for NACA.

Johnson worked at NASA for 33 years.

the other black people move to the back so white people could sit near the front. This experience made her more determined to succeed.

Johnson taught for many years. But she always wanted to do more. She heard that the National Advisory Committee for Aeronautics (NACA, later NASA) was hiring. It was looking specifically for black women to perform calculations. In the days before computers, these complex calculations were done by people. Johnson went to work for NACA in 1953. Her work was supposed to be basic. But she didn't see it that way. She asked questions, took on new duties, and worked her way up.

Johnson proved she could do more. When the United States decided to send men to the moon, she became a huge part of it. She had become an expert in geometry. She calculated the proper path that space rockets should take. Her calculations were used on America's first manned mission to space in 1961. She also worked on the first landing on the moon in 1969.

Johnson retired from NASA after 33 years in 1986. In her retirement, she spoke to students about the importance of studying science.

238,900
Approximate distance, in miles (384,472 km), from Earth to the moon.

- Johnson grew up counting things in her everyday life.
- She started teaching, but wanted to be a mathematician.
- She worked at NASA and helped calculate the flight path for spacecraft.

15

Lewis Latimer Assists Thomas Edison

Everybody knows Thomas Edison as one of the world's greatest inventors. But Edison did not do it alone. He had teams of brilliant scientists. These people also helped make life-changing inventions such as the light bulb. Lewis Latimer was one of those people.

Latimer was born the son of a runaway slave. His father, George, escaped six years before he was born. Latimer grew up hating slavery. When he was only 16, he joined the Union Army in the Civil War. After the war, he worked in the office of a patent lawyer. There, he became very good at drawing and understanding technology. He started work on his own inventions.

By 1874, he had a patent of his own. It was a bathroom designed for use on a train.

Latimer helped Edison improve the light bulb's design.

7

Number of patents Latimer was awarded in his lifetime.

- Latimer was the son of a runaway slave.
- He fought for the North during the Civil War.
- He first worked for a patent law firm, drawing blueprints, but soon was making his own inventions.
- He later worked with Thomas Edison and helped invent the light bulb.
- Latimer was an honored member of the Edison Pioneers, a club of men who had worked for Edison.

THINK ABOUT IT

Latimer had special knowledge that made him useful to Edison. How did Latimer's experience help Edison?

Latimer's knowledge of lighting and patent law was helpful to Edison. Latimer made sure nobody could copy Edison's designs. He helped Edison properly patent his work. In 1890, Latimer published a book on Edison's lighting system. It became a vital resource for electrical engineers. After working with Edison, Latimer went back to patent law.

In 1918, Latimer became a member of the Edison Pioneers. It was a new exclusive club of men who had worked with Edison. The goal of the group was to keep Edison's ideas alive. Latimer was an honored member, noted for his contributions to Edison's work and science.

Meanwhile, Latimer was also working more with electrical systems. In 1876, he drew up the blueprint for Alexander Graham Bell's telephone. Hiram Maxim hired Latimer in 1880 to work for his electric lighting company. But in 1884, Latimer caught the attention of Edison.

Jerry Lawson Helps Invent the Video Game Console

In the mid-1970s, most people didn't play video games at home. They had to go to an arcade. If they did have a home system, it played only one game. Jerry Lawson helped change all that.

As a boy, Lawson wanted to be a scientist. On his desk, he had a picture of George Washington Carver, another famous black inventor. Lawson grew up in New York. But in the early 1970s, he moved to California. There were many electronics companies just

The Channel F video game system used cartridges so that players could play different games on the same system.

starting then. Lawson joined a club for computer enthusiasts. Two of the other members were Steve Jobs and Steve Wozniak. Both men would go on to start Apple Computer.

Lawson was up to his own great things. He was in charge of a program at Fairchild Semiconductor to make a home video game console. But this one wouldn't play just one game like others of the time. It would come with different cartridges that each contained a game. Players could simply swap them out to play different games. Called the Channel F, it was the first one of its kind.

There were very few black men working in the video game industry. Even fewer were in charge of a whole department, like Lawson. There were soon other home consoles like Lawson's that hit the market. These sold better and became more famous than the Channel F. But they might not have happened without Lawson going first.

$22 billion

Approximate amount of money made by the video game industry in the United States in 2014.

- Lawson loved science as a boy.
- He moved to California to work in the electronics industry.
- Lawson was one of very few black men working in the video game industry.
- He designed the first video game console that had changeable games.

Lawson left his job in 1980. He founded his own video game company. Lawson passed away in 2011. But shortly before that, he was honored by the International Game Developers Association. He will be forever known as a pioneer in video game history.

10

Ada Lovelace: First Computer Programmer

Ada Lovelace's father was the famous poet Lord Byron. But her mother wanted her to study more practical things. Growing up in the early 1800s, Lovelace received an education in math, which she loved. It was unusual for a girl to study math. She had quite a gift for it.

In 1833, Lovelace met a man named Charles Babbage. He was a math professor at the University of Cambridge. Lovelace was only 17, but the two became friends over their shared interest in math and science. Babbage had developed a device called a "Difference Machine." It was an early example of a simple computer. Babbage showed this device to Lovelace. It got her thinking about what else computers could do.

Babbage began developing a new machine. It was bigger and better. Lovelace translated a French essay written by a mathematician about the machine. And she more than doubled its length with her own notes. She was able to describe exactly how the machine would work, if it were built. The computer would run on a series of punch cards. The order in which it processed the cards would lead to a certain action.

Lovelace's family encouraged her to study math.

Two pages of the new British passport design, unveiled in 2015, featured Charles Babbage and Lovelace.

Lovelace was able to detail one of these actions. For this reason, she is considered to have invented the first computer program. It was more than just math. It was a detailed process for a machine to follow. Today, she would be considered a computer programmer. Computer science did not exist at this time. Lovelace's work started people thinking about what computers could do.

As a woman in the 1800s, Lovelace received little credit for her work. People said she didn't really do the work. A man must have done it for her. But recently, Lovelace has been recognized for her achievements. October 13 is now Ada Lovelace Day around the world. It celebrates women in technology.

20,000
Number of words Lovelace wrote about Babbage's computer.

- Lovelace was educated in math and science.
- She met math professor Charles Babbage and became interested in computers.
- Her writings about a new kind of computer included the first computer program.

ADA THE COMPUTER LANGUAGE

In the late 1970s, the United States Department of Defense invented a new computer language. This language was unique because it brought together many different languages into one. It was given a fitting name: Ada.

Alan Turing Invents the Modern Computer

Alan Turing was always ahead of his time. Even in school as a boy, his mind raced. He loved science and had so many ideas he wanted to explore. School could not keep up with him. So he worked ahead on his own, dreaming of possibilities. His passion was mathematics. He was a superb student and attended Cambridge University on a full scholarship in 1935.

In 1936, Turing published a revolutionary paper. He thought of how humans performed tasks. He proposed a machine that could perform tasks in a similar way. Computers of that era had only one specific job. But Turing's machine could run any kind of program. It was still just an idea, however.

In 1939, Turing was called on for some very important work. His native Great Britain had entered World War II. To win the war, it needed help decoding enemy communications. Nazi Germany used a machine called the Enigma to make its messages impossible to read. Turing worked on figuring out how this machine worked.

He created a device that could go through all the billions of possible combinations of codes. It made the messages readable. The machine was gigantic. It ran all the time, figuring out messages. It turned out to be very effective. Turing even went to the United States to help the country with its own code breaking.

A statue of Turing stands on the University of Surrey campus in England.

150 quintillion

Number of possible combinations the German code machine could make.

- Turing was a math prodigy.
- He attended Cambridge on a full scholarship and became a prominent mathematician.
- He helped the British war effort by making a machine that could decode enemy messages.
- He also contributed to computer science by revolutionizing how computers think.

THE IMITATION GAME

Turing's achievements were not well known during his life. But in recent years, his contributions to technology have been revealed. In 2014, a film based on his code breaking work came out. *The Imitation Game* starred Benedict Cumberbatch as Turing. He was nominated for an Oscar. The film received eight Oscar nominations in all.

Turing's research was top secret. Nobody even knew it had been done until well after the war. But Turing's research would have an even greater impact. He was the first to consider how a computer "thinks." He based it on human behavior. This made computers more powerful. To him, he wasn't making a computer. He was making a model of the human brain.

Turing's contribution to World War II was kept secret until after the war.

James West Lets People Be Heard

James West learned a valuable lesson when he was eight years old. He was always interested in how things worked. If he didn't know, he'd take it apart to learn. One day, he had fixed a radio and tried to plug it in. The wiring was bad. He was hit with 120 volts of electricity. But instead of being scared, he was fascinated. He wanted to learn everything about electricity.

Growing up in the 1940s, West did not know many black men working in science. His father knew three men who had PhDs in chemistry or

West improved the microphones used in cell phones.

physics. But they could not get jobs in those areas. They worked at the post office. West's father did not want him going down that path. But West went to Temple University and graduated with a physics degree in 1957.

After college, West went to work for Bell Laboratories. There were only a few other black employees at Bell. He quickly showed himself to be one of the best minds there. He was brought on board for a special project. The microphones in telephones of that era needed to be improved. They wore out quickly and did not transmit sound well.

West used a technology that had been thought about since the 1700s. But its potential had not yet been understood. Called an electret, it did not lose quality or sensitivity over a long time. It was tiny and low cost. Today, this technology is used in 90 percent of microphones.

44
Number of years West worked for Bell Laboratories.

- Growing up, West took things apart to see how they worked.
- He went to work for Bell Laboratories, where he developed an improved microphone.
- West's microphone technology is still used in 90 percent of microphones today.
- He holds hundreds of other patents.

This is the most well known of West's inventions. But there are many others. His name is on 47 US patents and 200 others around the world. In 1999, he was inducted into the National Inventors Hall of Fame. He also worked as a professor at Johns Hopkins University.

Fact Sheet

- Lots of lower-tech inventions have also been made by some unsung heroes. The dishwasher was patented by a woman named Josephine Cochrane in 1886. Her first concern was not convenience, but that her dishes got chipped when washed by hand. In Cochrane's day, most houses did not have enough hot water to run such a machine. But with better technology in the 1940s, the invention took off.

- Women and minorities still lag behind in terms of technology careers. Google is one of the biggest tech companies in the world. As of 2014, just one percent of its workers were black. Two percent were Hispanic. Only 17 percent were women.

- The gas mask, which has saved countless lives from poison gas during wars, was invented by a black man named Garrett Morgan. He invented what he called a "breathing device" in 1914. It was originally intended to prevent the inhaling of smoke. Morgan also helped invent the modern traffic light. He added yellow to the standard lights of red and green.

- As of 2015, black people and Hispanic people still held far fewer jobs in the fields of science, technology, engineering, and mathematics than white people. Only six percent of workers in these fields were black. Approximately seven percent were Hispanic.

- In 1973, the National Inventors Hall of Fame was created. It honors people from all backgrounds who have made important contributions to technology and things we use every day. More than 500 inventors have been honored in its history. It is located just outside of Washington, DC, in Arlington, Virginia.

Glossary

cartridge
In video games, a cartridge is a single game that plugs into the console.

chemistry
The study of what things are made of.

geometry
A type of math dealing with shapes and lines.

laboratory
A place for research and scientific experiments.

laser
A beam of light sometimes used in medicine to cut things.

patent
Legal protection of an invention against it being copied.

physics
The study of physical sciences such as energy and force.

randomize
To put something in an unplanned order.

submarine
A watercraft that usually operates underwater.

telecommunications
Devices used for communicating, such as phones and faxes.

torpedo
A type of missile fired underwater.

transmit
To send something from one place to another.

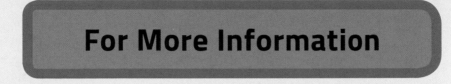

For More Information

Books

Davidson, Tish. *African American Scientists and Inventors*. Philadelphia, PA: Mason Crest, 2013.

Diehn, Andi. *Technology: Cool Women Who Code*. White River Junction, VT: Nomad Press, 2015.

Rowell, Rebecca. *The 12 Most Amazing American Inventions*. Mankato, MN: Peterson Publishing, 2015.

Visit 12StoryLibrary.com

Scan the code or use your school's login at **12StoryLibrary.com** for recent updates about this topic and a full digital version of this book. Enjoy free access to:

- Digital ebook
- Breaking news updates
- Live content feeds
- Videos, interactive maps, and graphics
- Additional web resources

Note to educators: Visit 12StoryLibrary.com/register to sign up for free premium website access. Enjoy live content plus a full digital version of every 12-Story Library book you own for every student at your school.

Index

Astro Electronics, 9

Babbage, Charles, 22
Bath, Patricia, 4–5
Bell Laboratories, 27
Bell Telephone, 13
Bose, Jagadish, 6–7
Brill, Yvonne, 8–9

cell phones, 17
Civil War, 18
code breaking, 24–25
computers, 10–11, 21,
    22–23, 24–25

Edison, Thomas, 18, 19

Hopper, Grace, 10–11

Jackson, Shirley Ann,
    12–13
Johnson, Katherine,
    14–15

Lamarr, Hedy, 16–17
Latimer, Lewis, 18–19
Lawson, Jerry, 20–21
Lovelace, Ada, 22–23

NASA, 9, 15
National Inventors Hall of
    Fame, 9, 27
Nobel Prize, 7

rocket science, 8–9

telecommunications, 13
Turing, Alan, 24–25

video games, 20–21

West, James, 26–27
wireless telegraph, 7
World War II, 8, 10,
    16–17, 24–25

About the Author

Todd Kortemeier is a writer from Minneapolis, Minnesota. He is a graduate of the University of Minnesota's School of Journalism & Mass Communication. He has authored many books for young people.

READ MORE FROM 12-STORY LIBRARY

Every 12-Story Library book is available in many formats. For more information, visit 12StoryLibrary.com.